BOOK 3
Short -i

The Fishing Trip

ISBN: 978-1-338-57286-5

10 9 8 7 6 5 4 3 2 1   19 20 21 22 23

Printed in Malaysia   106

First printing, 2019

Book design by Marissa Asuncion

Scholastic Inc.

Woody and Jessie
take a **trip**.
They go down by the **river**
to catch some **fish**.

The Prospector
is at the **river**, too.
He **is** looking for gold.
If there **is** gold
in the **river**,
he **will** find **it**!

The Prospector
dips his pan
in the water.
He **sifts** out **bits** of sand
and rock.
There **is** no gold **in** the pan.
Looking for gold can be **tricky**.

The Prospector
sees Woody.
"Any **fish** yet?"
says the Prospector.
"Not yet," says Woody.

Just then, the Prospector sees a **bit** of gold **in** the water. He jumps **in** the **river** after **it**!

The Prospector wants to
catch the **little bits** of gold.
He **grips his** hat
and lets the water **spill in**.
"I'm gonna be **rich**!" he says.

Woody forgets about catching a **fish**.
He jumps **in** the **river** to help catch the **little bits** of gold.

Jessie sees her friends **in** the river. Their hats are wet and full of gold **bits**. "We're gonna be **rich**!" says the Prospector.

Jessie smiles.
"Yes, you will be **rich**,"
she says.
"**Rich with** gold **fish**!"